MW01679535

Hellfighters Operations Manual 2

The Commission of a Hellfighter

HELLFIGHTERS OPERATIONS MANUAL 2

The Commission of a Hellfighter

RICHARD W. HEADRICK

HELLFIGHTER PUBLICATIONS

Copyright © 2008 by Richard W. Headrick

Published by Hellfighter Publications

One Freedom Square, Laurel, MS 39440-3367

All rights reserved. Printed and bound in the United States of America. This book or parts thereof may not be reproduced in any form, stored in a retrieval system, or transmitted in any form by any means – electronic, mechanical, photocopy, recording, or otherwise – without prior written permission of the publisher, except as provided by United States of America copyright law.

Unless otherwise noted, all Scripture quotations are from the King James Version of the Bible.

Scripture quotations marked NKJV are taken from the New King James Version® of the Bible. Copyright © 1982 by Thomas Nelson, Inc. Used by permission. All rights reserved.

Scripture quotations marked NASB are taken from the New American Standard Bible®, Copyright © 1960, 1962, 1963, 1968, 1971, 1972, 1973, 1975, 1977, 1995 by The Lockman Foundation. Used by permission. (www.lockman.org)

Scripture quotations marked NIV are taken from the HOLY BIBLE, NEW INTERNATIONAL VERSION®. NIV®. Copyright© 1973, 1978, 1984 by International Bible Society. Used by permission of Zondervan. All rights reserved.

Scripture quotations marked NLT are taken from the Holy Bible, New Living Translation®, copyright © 1996 by Tyndale Charitable Trust. Used by permission of Tyndale House Publishers. All rights reserved.

ISBN 978-0-9787573-1-1

Library of Congress Control Number 2008932870

Book design by SeedStudios.com

Back cover photo by Matt "Upshot" Miller

When you go to war against your enemies... and see... an army greater than yours, do not be afraid of them, because the Lord your God... will be with you.

Deuteronomy 20:1 (NIV)

The Cover

The Commission of a Hellfighter is an invigorating challenge for all of mankind, but only the strongest will rise to the great calling. A calling that requires a belief in the all-powerfulness of God. A calling that mandates a faith that people can change. A calling that demands a radical strengthening of your spirit. *The Commission of a Hellfighter* is only for those who will humble themselves to the life-changing power of the One who can change everything.

Remember God sends His angelic servants, like the one depicted on the cover of this book, to fight with you and strengthen your spirit. Submitted to the power and authority of Almighty God, nothing can stop a Hellfighter!

Appreciation

For almost 40 years, Terry Busbea has been Art Director for our company. Without exception, every project he has ever created has been a true masterpiece and, no matter what it took to make it happen, he has never missed a deadline.

Terry "Buzz" Busbea was instrumental in the initial development and launch of the Hellfighters series. Without him, it would not have been possible.

Additional thanks to Russell Lake and his team at Seed Studios for their creative input and bringing to fruition this ambitious project.

Dedication

If anyone knows about spiritual warfare, it's Mike Shirley. He joined forces with the enemy in his youth and fought alongside Satan's comrades of evil until Jesus saved his soul in 2000. It was then that Mike received *The Commission* to do great things for God.

Today, Mike Shirley is an extraordinary Hellfighter who loves to serve Jesus Christ.

It's because of Mike's great love for Jesus that we dedicate this *Hellfighters Operations Manual* to him.

Contents

Be ye therefore ready also: for the Son of man cometh at an hour ye think not.

Luke 12:40

Introduction

Well, well, well, I see you've got your orange vest of commitment on. Good for you! I'm so proud you've decided to accept the exciting challenge and awesome responsibility of becoming a Hellfighter.

Compared to the whole of humanity there aren't a lot of us, but there are more now since you've joined God's League of Extraordinary Ladies and Gentlemen. I believe that you bring with you a desire and commitment to make a difference.

This *Hellfighters Operations Manual 2: The Commission of a Hellfighter* will help you discover what your responsibility as a Hellfighter really is.

In the military branches of our government, promotions play an important role in the career of a soldier, sailor or airman. If, for example, a soldier never gets promoted from buck private to, let's say, sergeant, he will forever be a doer of small things: a grunt, a jarhead or canon fodder; expendable, as my dad used to say.

A Christian is a buck private in God's army and will never amount to much of anything either unless he strives to do so. A Hellfighter, however, rises through the ranks in God's army and becomes as a commissioned officer.

A Hellfighter is a bold and courageous leader. Why? Because he's prepared for his mission. He has trained by studying God's Word, talking to God regularly and doing for others as he would have others do for him. A Hellfighter wants to be just like Jesus, not a pew-warmer like most Christians.

To help you become the best Hellfighter you can be, we've prepared a few rules for engaging the enemy. These rules will reinforce your commission as a leader in God's army.

By honoring God's Word and applying a few "tricks of the trade," your successes will be recorded by the names of those you recruit. *The Commission of a Hellfighter* will help to confirm that you do have what it takes to accomplish your mission for Jesus. It will also teach you how to grow in strength and wisdom as you totally commit yourself to God's mission for your life.

By reading this *Hellfighters Operations Manual*, you have revealed your desire to serve the King of kings to an even higher degree than you ever thought possible. You have also sealed your commitment to exercise your faith and raise high your banner for Christ. You have decisively made a commitment to neither sit nor stand still, but to lead other soldiers in God's army to victory.

A Hellfighter's goal, however, is not just victory; it is to bring about the total annihilation of all the demons of hell including, but not limited to, that old serpent, that old dragon, that old destroyer of men's souls... Satan himself.

Jesus said in Matthew 16:18b *...I will build My church; and the gates of hell shall not prevail against it.* We Hellfighters are the "it" in that verse because we are the church. Since my wife's name is Gina, I'll personalize this verse for her, "the gates of hell shall not prevail against Gina." Now you can personalize it for yourself, "the gates of hell shall not prevail against ________________."
(write your name here)

I'm serious, brother, that verse is talking about you and me so LET'S GO GETTUM! Let's tear those "gates of hell" off their hinges and tear the devil's strongholds down. I'll do my part! Will you do your part? If we will, then others will and before you know it, we Hellfighters can change the world for Christ. Sounds great, doesn't it?

To some degree, it sounds a little too easy. But you know what? It should be easy. If every child of God who truly believes that Jesus came, died, rose again and is coming back would do what we are commanded to do in Matthew 28:19, 20, we could change the world.

Matthew 28:19, 20 is not a suggestion or a recommendation; it's a command from our Sovereign God and we had better resign ourselves to the fact that it's up to me and you to carry it out.

To be a great Hellfighter, you must memorize this Scripture and put it to use daily, *"Go therefore and make disciples of all nations, baptizing them in the name of the Father and of the Son and of the Holy Spirit, teaching them to observe all things that I have commanded you; and lo, I am with you always, even to the end of the age." Amen* (Matthew 28:19, 20, NKJV).

We touched on this in our first *Hellfighters Operations Manual, The Call of a Hellfighter*, and we'll probably touch on it again in this and other *Operations Manuals*. It's important that we understand the gravity of what I'm about to say. If the Christian community would rise up off their "blessed assurances" and stop wasting their time watching mindless TV, reading worthless magazines, and surfing the Net, we could make a difference. If the Christian community would tithe as they should instead of spending their money on things they don't need to impress people they don't know, then we would be an unstoppable army. But, you know what? Most folks really don't give a hoot if you, or anyone else for that matter, go to hell.

To be honest, most folks really don't care if their own mama, daddy, brother or sister go to hell. In today's society for instance, the majority of people just don't concern themselves with such things anymore. The philosophy of our day and age is just like that of Noah—eat, drink and be merry, baby, it's party time!

The "do anything" lifestyle seemed to work pretty well for Noah's generation and they got by with it until it started raining. However, that little shower sure messed up the party and everybody died, except Noah and his family. Our nation, too, is becoming a godless society, and it is evident that the lifestyles of most Americans are very similar to those of the people who lived during the days of Noah.

Gina and I recently returned from Key West, Florida. Never before had we seen such blatant, and shockingly public, displays of immorality. What we witnessed was a scene reminiscent of what Sodom and Gomorrah must have been like. Areas such as this, in our own country, will be the targets of God's wrath, just like Sodom and Gomorrah were.

I believe that one day soon it will start raining again. I know He promised not to use "sky juice" again to destroy mankind, but it's very likely that some rogue nation will "rain" hundreds of missiles down on us, and that, my friend, would once again spoil the party. It would also sentence millions of unbelievers to hell because we, who call ourselves Christians, have failed to fulfill the great commission of Matthew 28:19, 20 (NKJV), *"Go therefore and make disciples of all nations* [America included], *baptizing them in the name of the Father and of the Son and of the Holy Spirit, teaching them to observe all things that I have commanded you; and lo, I am with you always, even to the end of the age." Amen.*

This is where we Hellfighters come in. It's up to us to get the lead out and tell everyone we meet about Jesus. I'm ready to "Go Gettum!" *Are you?* I'm ready to pay the price, whatever it takes! *Are you?* I'm willing to get up earlier, stay up later, read my Bible more, pray more, witness more and do more for Christ than I've ever done before.

Are you? By doing so, I'll be better prepared to introduce Jesus to as many men, women, boys and girls as I can. **Are you prepared?**

Will you, too, join the ranks of those valiant heroes of the faith who came before us? It would be an insult for us to let them down. It would also be an insult to the One who died for us not to give it all we've got. Amen?

We must commit to memory the meaning of the word *witness*. This is how the dictionary defines *witness*: [1]One who has seen or heard something; [2]something that serves as evidence; [3]a sign; [4]to testify.

We must be willing to exercise its meaning without any hint of compromise or hesitation. Why? Because Hellfighters don't just defend...we attack!

The Bible is the ultimate guidebook and instruction manual for us to follow, but sometimes it's difficult to understand. This *Hellfighters Operations Manual* puts some of God's rules that pertain to our effectiveness for Him in layman's terms. A child can understand this little book. So whether you're a non-believer, an immature

Believer or a champion of the faith, sit down, get comfortable and bone up on how you can be a wonderful blessing to others.

ATTACK...
DON'T JUST DEFEND!

I will meditate
on Your precepts,
And contemplate
Your ways,
I will delight
myself in Your
statutes;
I will not forget
Your Word.

Psalm 119:15, 16 (NKJV)

RULE #1

Never Take God for Granted

My sister, Janet, told me many years ago, "Start your day with Jesus early in the morning and He will be with you all day long." I think that's good advice, don't you?

I am, however, guilty, as I suspect you are, of not spending enough time on my knees. As bad as I hate to admit it, I fall short in conversing with my Heavenly Father as often as I should.

I know in my heart that He's always there and will always take time for me whenever I get ready to spend a little time with Him. But, that doesn't give any of us the right to take Him for granted.

How preposterous for a man or woman to even think that the God of all creation is just hanging around twiddling His thumbs, waiting for some little insignificant human being like you or me, to take a minute and say "hello" to Him.

God is God. God is the great I Am. God is the One and only, omnipresent being of the universe. He is also omnipotent and quite able to make it on His own, whether we take two minutes to say "hello" to Him or not. But you know what? Even in His greatness, He waits patiently for you and me to say "hello" to Him in the morning and "goodnight" to Him in the evening. We should, however, be very considerate of His time and we should be very considerate of the way we approach Him.

Even though He is waiting patiently for us to say "hello," how heartbreaking it must be for Him to know that the only time you or I say "hello," is when we *want* something—prosperity, stuff, protection, health, etc. Wouldn't it be nice from time to time to simply say, "Hello, Lord. How are You today? Is everything going okay? Can I do anything for You? Is there something I can help You with, Lord? What's my mission today? I'm ready to serve You, please use me. Jesus, I just want You to know how much I love You. I can never thank You enough for Your grace and Your mercy. I will never stop praising You for Your goodness toward me."

When we talk to God, we should be reporting for duty and singing His praises, not asking for a handout.

We treat Him as followers of many religions treat their idols. They keep them on a shelf, on the dash of their car, in their pocket or around their neck, so those who have been deceived by these devilish cults can access their gods anytime it's convenient for them. Don't we do the same thing to our great God Jehovah, the Creator of everything? What blatant disrespect we show to our Heavenly Father!

Don't get me wrong; I know that the Bible says in 1 Thessalonians 5:17 that we are to *Pray without ceasing*. And to do so means we will be approaching God's throne to talk with Him about some pretty strange things. But, you know what? God cares about our every need and therefore expects us to come to Him seeking assistance, guidance and wisdom. And He can handle that alright. Just don't get so complacent and lackadaisical that you take Him for granted by thinking He's the Heavenly Thrift Store where you can get everything you want for free!

To take the Creator of all things for granted would be the highest form of insult. It would be contempt in its rudest form, so let's pray to and praise the God of Creation so often and so reverently that He will be happy to hear from us, no matter what.

If we'll just report for duty unreservedly and allow Him to direct our steps each day, there is no telling what He would allow us to learn. I've got a hunch He would *...show you great and mighty things, which you do not know* (Jeremiah 33:3b, NKJV).

Just remember this: the more you pray and honor God, the more ticked off Satan will become. Why? Because Satan doesn't like you. As a matter of fact, he has never liked you and to be perfectly honest he hates your guts.

ATTACK… DON'T JUST DEFEND!

THE THIEF DOES NOT COME EXCEPT TO STEAL, AND TO KILL, AND TO DESTROY...

JOHN 10:10A (NKJV)

RULE #2

Remember, Satan Hates Your Guts

You're not the one who does the saving of men's souls, Jesus is. The Bible plainly says in Luke 19:10, *For the Son of Man is come to seek and to save that which was lost.* Satan, on the other hand, wants to destroy every man, woman, boy and girl on planet earth. How do I know that? Because in 1 Peter 5:8b the Bible says, *...your adversary the devil, as a roaring lion, walketh about, seeking whom he may devour.* Jesus came to save and the devil came to destroy; therefore, Satan is obviously our enemy. He will not, however, attack you openly at first. He is sneaky like a snake and cunning like a fox. He will, however, pounce on you like a wild animal when you least expect it.

When I was in my twenties, I did some business with a man who owned a "tourist trap" called *Adventure Land* on the Mississippi Gulf Coast. He had souvenirs galore and a zoo that contained exotic animals from around the world.

One day I called on him and he said he was too busy to see me, but if I wanted to kill an hour or two in his zoo he would see me later. Being a salesman and wanting to keep this man's business, I decided to go see the animals which, by the way, I had seen many times before.

As I made my way to the jaguar cages, I passed other ferocious animals. The cages were not made of steel bars; no, sir, nothing but "chicken wire" separated me from the animals. If, however, those protective barriers, as skimpy as they were, had not been there, I would probably not be here today.

When I got to the jaguar cages, I could not see any of my "friends." The camouflage, which God provided them with, was concealing them perfectly. I eased closer to the fence until my toes touched it. I then lifted my hands and arms about head high. I reached out and put my fingers through the protective wire barricade. Then stupidity took over; I pressed my face against the wire so I could see more clearly. Oh, I saw clearly alright! In an instant, a jaguar, which had been lying perfectly hidden no more than 3 or 4 feet from me, lunged and matched my position on the fence barricade. There we stood face-to-face, hand-to-paw and foot-to-paw. That was a moment when the expression "peed in your pants" almost became a reality.

Good gracious, man, that nearly scared me to death! I mean, in an instant, he was on me. But, Bubba, let me tell you this. I set the world speed record for backing up. It seemed as if my feet had little rockets in them.

Satan is just like that old jaguar. He knows the things you like. He knows what you want to see, feel, and enjoy, and when you give in to his temptations, BAM! He pounces on you like a ravenous beast. He seeks to devour you. He seeks to ruin you and he seeks to diminish your dreams. He seeks to snatch from your grasp the wonderful life God has in store for you and he will, if you let him. So, remember this if you don't remember anything else I say in this book, SATAN HATES YOUR GUTS! 1 Peter 5:8b says, *...because your adversary the devil, as a roaring lion, walketh about, seeking whom he may devour.* Satan hates your guts and will do everything in his power to discredit you and destroy you if God will let him.

When you made your commitment to become a Hellfighter, did you have any idea of the odds you were going to be up against? Are you still as courageous as you were before you became a Hellfighter, or are you a wuss who is ready to chicken out? Look intently at the following scenario and see what you would do:

A fight breaks out between two men and a woman in front of your church. Let's pretend that this woman has been dating these two men at the same time. The day has come for her to make a decision. She tells one of them that she will go with the other. One suitor is infuriated. He rants and raves, and becomes abusive to the woman. The winner of her affection, in an effort to defend her and prove his love for her, takes his position between the love of his life and her angry suitor.

The battle begins—fists fly, sickening sounds of broken bones and ripped flesh fill your ears. Blood flows as the battle rages for the love of this woman, while you and the other church-goers stand and watch. Why doesn't someone do something? Why don't you intervene? The woman is trying to break it up, but she's too frail. Here all of you are—big, strong church-goers, protectors of the right—yet you do nothing, except stand there and watch. Or maybe you do the American thing and look the other way.

Chances are, very few onlookers, if any, would get involved. The popular reasoning would be, "It's not our problem, so it doesn't concern us." What would you do? Would you make it your business?

You see, oh faithful member of the Scaredy Cat Club, furious battles for the souls of lost men are raging all around us at this very minute and most

Christians are doing nothing, except looking the other way.

The demons of hell are fighting the angels of Heaven for the souls of men, women, boys and girls, while most Christians do nothing. In fact, the Christian community as a whole acts as if nothing is going on. The demons of hell have been instructed by their commander in chief to entice and ensnare as many unsuspecting victims as they can, yet most Christians simply look the other way as friends, and strangers alike, go to hell.

The Captain of Heaven's mighty army is Jesus. In Joshua 5:14, 15 we read, *And He said, Nay; but as Captain of the host of the Lord am I now come. And Joshua fell on his face to the earth, and did worship, and said unto Him, What saith my lord unto His servant? And the Captain of the Lord's host said unto Joshua, Loose thy shoe from off thy foot; for the place whereon thou standest is holy. And Joshua did so.*

He has directed the angels of Heaven to engage the enemy and withdraw from their grip those lost and hell-bound sinners who are struggling to free themselves from Satan's grasp. But where are you, sir? Are you in the foxhole of fear or on the frontlines of the battle?

Can you imagine the battle that was waged for your soul? I know the battle that was waged for mine. I wanted to saddle up with Jesus when I was thirteen, but I didn't. The story of my salvation experience is found in my book, *Goliath's Fall*. It took 47 years for the valiant and tenacious angels of Heaven, led by Jesus, the "Hound of Heaven," to free me from Satan's hideous grasp. Are you free yet?

Let me clarify something before we go any further. I told you earlier that you and I can't save anybody. Neither can the angels; however, they protect us from death until Jesus is ready for us to come home. In Psalm 91:11 the Bible says, *For He shall give His angels charge over thee, to keep thee in all thy ways.*

My angel brothers gave 47 years of their existence protecting me and keeping me alive so Jesus could save me, and I haven't taken their sacrifice lightly.

Had I given my heart to Jesus when I was 13, I would have been spared a lot of misery. I would not have had to experience the wild side of life; the adventures into the dark side of worldly lust; and the expeditions into the depths of heathen cultures. I would not have had to fight my battles alone. I would have neither scars nor memories of my defeats.

However, had I given my heart to Jesus when I was 13, I might have grown up to be a plain-Jane, vanilla-wrapped Christian who goes to church on Sunday mornings and when church is over says, "Well, my obligation for this week is done. See you next week, Jesus." Luke 7:47b (NASB) says it so profoundly, *"... he who is forgiven little, loves little."* On the contrary, I was forgiven a LOT! Therefore, I love Him a LOT! I am so thankful that God saved me and I hope I never get over it! *...Save us, O God of our salvation, and gather us together, and deliver us from the heathen, that we may give thanks to Thy holy name, and glory in Thy praise* (1 Chronicles 16:35).

What about the battle for your soul? Was it one where the angels earned their money, or were you one of the blessed ones, like my wife, Gina? God allowed her to be saved at an early age. Perhaps you were like Gina and did not have to endure a life of hellacious living? Praise God if you were! Praise God also if your life was a living hell, because now you can thank Him for allowing you to become a Hellfighter!

It's not important how old you were when you accepted Jesus, the important thing is that you never get over it! *At midnight I will rise to give thanks unto Thee*... (Psalm 119:62a).

Let me emphasize one more time that *you* can't save anyone, neither can the Heavenly realm of angels; not Michael, the warring angel, not even Gabriel, the gatekeeper of Heaven, can save anyone. Only the precious Lamb of God can save a soul from hell.

With all that said, remember this: We don't do the saving, but we are responsible for introducing our Redeemer to those who are lost. In other words, we're to be a good spokesperson.

ATTACK... DON'T JUST DEFEND!

GOD THUNDERETH MARVELOUSLY WITH HIS VOICE; GREAT THINGS DOETH HE, WHICH WE CANNOT COMPREHEND.

JOB 37:5

RULE #3

Be a Good Spokesperson

Have you ever been to some big gala where the featured guest was introduced in a way that was so impressive and informative that you felt you knew the guy, but since you didn't, you sure wanted to? I have, but I've also been to some events where, had I been the guest speaker, I would have been embarrassed, to say the least, by the introduction.

You and I are to be introducers of the most featured guest of all time, Jesus Christ. We, as Hellfighters, have been given this awesome responsibility of introducing the King of kings to everyone, everywhere.

Now listen to this, not only does Jesus want to meet your friends, but He wants to come live with those you introduce Him to. So, make sure your walk with God is close enough, your study of the Bible deep enough, your prayer life powerful enough and your relationship with Jesus intimate enough to be able to give your lost friends an introduction that will both impress and compel them to accept our Lord Jesus Christ as their personal Savior.

If your walk with God is irregular, your study of the Bible shallow and your prayer life so weak that you can't tell a lost friend or even a stranger who Jesus really is, then it's time to get up off your duff and start studying. 2 Timothy 2:15 says, *Study to shew thyself approved unto God, a workman that needeth not to be ashamed, rightly dividing the Word of truth*. A recent survey showed that 85% of church attendees could not lead a dying family member, or anyone else for that matter, to Christ if asked to do so.

As a Hellfighter; as a born again Believer in Jesus Christ; as a Bible-toting, praise-song-singing, bent-knee-praying, and uncompromising purveyor of the truths of Almighty God, I say unto you what God's Word says in Matthew 3:17 when God the Father introduces His Son to us for the first time: *This is My beloved Son in whom I am well pleased*. That's a great introduction, don't you think? But there's much more that we can say about Jesus.

Delve deep into the Old Testament and you'll find the shadows of Christ reflected in its pages. Delve deep into the New Testament and you'll find His glorious light reflecting far into eternity.

To be a good spokesperson and to make the proper introduction of Jesus, you will need to spend a lot of time in God's Holy Word. You must learn everything that will allow you to introduce Jesus as the most miraculous entity ever to grace the presence of man.

In Genesis, He is the *Creator* of everything. In the story of Noah, He is the *Ark* of Salvation. In Exodus,

He is the *Deliverer* of His people. In Joshua, He is the *Captain* of the hosts. In Psalms, He is the *Son, Shepherd, Savior* and *King*. In Proverbs, He is *Wisdom*. In Isaiah, He is the *Lamb* led to the slaughter, yet triumphs as our glorious Messiah. In Daniel, He closed the mouths of lions. In the story of Shadrach, Meshach and Abednego, He's the *Fourth* man in the fiery furnace. In Matthew, He's the *King* of the Jews. In Mark, He's the *Servant* of Jehovah. In Luke, He's the *Son* of Man. In John, He's the *Son* of God. In Philippians, He is the *Supplier* of our needs. In Colossians, He is *Pre-eminent*. In 1 Timothy He is our *Mediator* between God and Man. In 2 Timothy, He is our *Judge*. In James, He is our *Healer*. In 2 John, He *prospers* our souls. In Jude, He is our *Savior* and only wise God. In Revelation, He is our soon coming *King*.

Now, how's that for an introduction? Want more? Listen to this:

In the Gospels, we can read about His miracles, listen to His parables, and watch Him bestow unmerited love and favor to everyone He meets. He is no respecter of persons. Everyone, and I do mean everyone, is equal in His sight.

In Matthew 13 He is found as a *Sower* of seeds, a *Merchant* selling pearls, and a *Man* who finds treasure in his own fields. In the story of the ninety and nine found in Matthew 18, He is the *Good Shepherd*. In Matthew 25, we read about Him as the ultimate *Judge* in the story of the sheep and the goats. Also in Matthew 25 we find Him as the *Bridegroom* in the story of the wise and foolish virgins. In Luke 10, He is found as the *Good Samaritan* on the Jericho Road. He is *Prophet, Priest and King*. He is the *Way,* the *Truth* and the *Life*. He's the *Cornerstone* of the church. He's the *Rock of Ages*. He's Paul's blinding *Light* on the Damascus Road and He's the *Earthquake* that opened the doors of the Philippian jail. He's the *Rose of Sharon*, the *Bright and Morning Star*, and the *Fairest* of ten thousand. He's our sacrificial *Lamb* who rode into Jerusalem the first time on a borrowed donkey. But when He returns one day, accompanied by the Hosts of Heaven, He'll be riding a white stallion and on His cape and on His thigh will be emblazoned *KING OF KINGS AND LORD OF LORDS!*

Does that get your adrenaline flowing or what? Son!!! Can you picture that? Even a Steven Spielberg movie could not begin to compare with the powerful pomp and circumstance that will herald the coming of King Jesus, the Christ of Calvary.

I want to be with Him when He comes, but at the same time, I would love to be here to see His coming. I can't figure out where the best vantage point will be, from the ground looking up and seeing Heaven open, or with the Saints as they gallop through the portals of Heaven's glory and enter triumphantly into the realm of earth. I kind of think the latter, because I want to watch Satan as he scurries about trying to find a place to hide. You do know he's a coward don't you? He professes to be a bad dude and I won't challenge that. In fact, I believe he's the worst dude there has ever been. A formidable foe to the Hosts of Heaven, but in the end… he's dead meat! It's just a matter of time.

As Hellfighters, we will definitely be with Jesus when He returns, and I really don't think that will be long. If you're reading this in any year after

2008, His coming is a lot nearer than when this book was written. So you had better get ready, brother. His coming is just around the corner. Maybe even tonight!

Do you have enough background information to put together a good introduction for Jesus? I purposely left off the Scripture references for some of the passages we used. It will mean more to you if you have to research and dig 'em out yourself.

During my Bible study time, I use *Matthew Henry's Commentary*, *Willmington's Guide to the Bible* and other "help books" that aid me in understanding more about God's Word. But, remember this, don't get so caught up in the "help books" that you forget *The Book* from which all Christian "help books" are written.

This Rule, *Be a Good Spokesperson*, encourages you to make a good first impression, and in this case, a good first introduction. Everything you need to know to introduce Jesus properly is in your Bible; you simply have to find it. Jesus plainly says in Luke 11:9, *...Ask, and it shall be given you; seek, and ye shall find; knock, and it shall be opened* *unto you.* I believe Him, don't you? 2 Timothy 2:15 says, *Study to shew thyself approved unto God, a workman that needeth not to be ashamed, rightly dividing the Word of truth.* Simple, huh?

The intensity with which you seek Christ's mysteries and His history will be governed by the amount of fizz in your Coca-Cola faith. If you let a Coke sit open for a little while, it will soon lose its fizz. Even we Hellfighters can lose our fizz if we don't stay focused on God's Word. Matthew 5:13 (NKJV) warns, *"You are the salt of the earth; but if the salt loses its flavor, how shall it be seasoned? It is then good for nothing but to be thrown out and trampled underfoot by men."*

The Bible says in Exodus 20:3 (NKJV), *"You shall have no other gods before Me."* TV, Internet, newspapers, magazines, work, sports, etc. will all take precedence over our study of God's Word if we aren't careful. So, don't get lulled into letting your guard down. Remember, Satan hates your guts and he wants you to fail, big time. He wants your enemies to rejoice in your failures, so don't give them a chance. Hellfighters must stay close to God's Word and if we will stay close to Him, He will stay close to us.

Most Christians have many gods. But, Hellfighters (a.k.a. Coca-Cola Christians) only serve the One true God. His name is Jehovah!

ATTACK... DON'T JUST DEFEND!

...THE LORD WILL GIVE GRACE AND GLORY; NO GOOD THING WILL HE WITHHOLD FROM THEM THAT WALK UPRIGHTLY.

PSALM 84:11B

Rule #4

Be a Coca-Cola Christian

When I was a young man, the quality and taste of all soft drinks was compared to Coca-Cola. Worldwide marketing boasted Coca-Cola as being "The Real Thing."

I think the Christian community could learn a lot from those Christians who are "The Real Thing." Problem is, there are only a few real ones. I call them Coca-Cola Christians.

For the most part, our churches are filled with "Sunday morning" Christians. However, some churches are sprinkled with a few hellfighting, tried and true, Coca-Cola Christians, who, if asked, could without hesitation, introduce Jesus to anyone as the One and only Son of God.

2 Timothy 2:15 says, *Study to shew thyself approved unto God, a workman that needeth not to be ashamed, rightly dividing the Word of truth.*

This is a plain-Jane, vanilla-wrapped verse. You don't need to be a Cambridge Bible scholar to unwrap the intricate mysteries of it because there is no mystery to it at all. All you have to do is take it for face value. Study God's Word like you should, and then you can tell people the truths that lie within its pages. Simple, huh!

You don't have to be a scholar; you don't have to have a college degree. In fact, you don't even have to have a formal education to read and understand God's Word, all you have to do is be born again. Nowadays you don't even need to be able to read. You can buy the Bible on CD and listen to its revelations.

Some of God's greatest soulwinners have not been highly educated, but they have been highly inquisitive about the Bible and because of their love for God and their inquisitiveness and aspirations to learn more about Him, they became self-taught students of God's Word. God even told me one time, "Richard, I'll let you know all you *want* to know." In other words, "It's in the Book, Richard, but you're gonna have to read and study it before I'll let you in on its great and mighty secrets." The same goes for you.

I love to hear the learned scholars of God's Word present the Gospel, but I'm glad I got to hear the old time "camp meeting" preachers of yesterday. Those were the guys who stepped on the toes of sinners. There are still some preachers, big and small alike, who preach the hellfire and damnation sermons of yesteryear, but they are few and far between. It's sad, but true that there are very few left in that brigade of pulpit-pounding, rafter-raising, foot-stomping, devil-hating preachers. Most have died and gone to be with the Lord.

Many of America's theological seminaries and Bible colleges have, for the most part, gone the way of the world, allowing liberal professors who are sympathetic to every cause, except those that are righteous, to teach our students watered down Biblical truths. I'm gonna "park here for a minute," as Harold Danley would say.

Exceptions to the above statement include the following seminary presidents: Dr. Paige Patterson at Southwestern Seminary in Fort Worth; Dr. Chuck Kelly at New Orleans Seminary; Dr. Phil Roberts at Midwestern Seminary in Kansas City; and Dr. Mike Spradlin at Mid-America Seminary in Memphis. These capable presidents are leading a new regiment of godly scholars to teach and mentor their students scripturally.

Dr. Danny Akin, president of Southeastern Seminary in Wake Forest, North Carolina, is another godly leader who recognizes the fact that the church's decline can be partially blamed on men like him.

He said one day in a seminary chapel service, "Our churches are declining because pastors are not being properly trained, simply because those who are doing the training are doing a poor job of it. If our seminary educators are doing a poor job then the blame lies on our seminary presidents and that means THE BUCK STOPS HERE."

What a powerful admission of failure on the part of academia. What courage Danny Akin has to speak such truths publicly.

To prove Dr. Akin's profound statement to be true, I will share with you some sobering facts. Harvard University, founded in 1636 as Harvard College, is the oldest and most prestigious institution of higher learning in the United States. It was named after John Harvard, a young minister. Harvard started out right and the majority of its early graduates became ministers. In fact, for the first 70 years of the school's existence all the presidents were conservative clergymen.

Do you think for a second that those original students and faculty members would have ever dreamed that their beloved Harvard could possibly turn into the ultra-liberal, breeding ground for Christian-haters that it is today? I seriously doubt it.

The scary part is that Harvard is educating over 30,000 students each year and brain-washing them in the process into believing there is no God and that we Christians are the bad guys. The same thing is happening on countless other college and university campuses around the world. These students are the ones being groomed to be our next generation of local, state, national and world leaders.

As Hellfighters, we must take note. The enemy is unleashing a whole new, vicious breed of antagonists and we have to be prepared to take them on, whether one on one or as a group. We must be prepared and ready to defend our faith—to prove the truth of Christianity—without wavering. The proper term for this is called *apologetics,* which comes from the Greek word *apologia* meaning *defense of a position against an attack*. Hellfighters need to be proficient in apologetics.

Now, I have to be very honest with you. I don't like using the word *apologetics* in association with the word *Hellfighters* because I'm afraid someone is going to get confused and mistakenly think I'm asking you to be apologetic (to express an apology or regret) for defending your faith. No way! The two words are as different as night and day! Let the record show: Hellfighters should never *apologize* for sharing the Gospel with a lost world or for standing up for the cause of Christ! Only Christian cowards do that.

Atheists and agnostics don't apologize for their disbelief in our Creator God. Alcoholics don't apologize for getting drunk. Prostitutes don't apologize for being whores. Beer drinkers, cigarette smokers, snuff dippers, tobacco chewers and drug addicts don't apologize for their convictions, so why should we apologize for ours? Those who are anti-Christ don't apologize for being opposed to the things of Christ. So why should we apologize for being opposed to the things of Satan? We shouldn't, yet some Believers do. It's as if they're afraid to offend anyone, or at least that's what counterfeit Christians say.

Counterfeit Christians, who profess to be something they're not, will usually say when an opportunity to witness comes along, "Oh, I would tell so and so about Christ, but I'm afraid I might offend them by talking to them about Christianity."

Hellfighters don't care if they offend an already hell-bound sinner with an evangelistic tribute to an almighty God. Hellfighters tell the story of God's love and mercy to everyone. When a Hellfighter really commits to serving the Lord Jesus Christ, it becomes their passion.

Counterfeit Christians are afraid of offending lost folks because they're one of them. They're weak, jelly-bellied, pew-warming, Sunday morning, lip-serving, wannabe soulwinners who are actually hell-bound sinners. They wouldn't know enough Scripture to present Jesus to an uninformed person, even if they were saved. Once again, I want to emphasize 2 Timothy 2:15, *Study to shew thyself approved unto God, a workman that needeth not to be ashamed, rightly dividing the Word of truth*.

It's sad to say, but most Christians are in the same boat as the counterfeit Christians. Without God's power, a Christian can't be an effective soulwinner either! I'll repeat 2 Timothy 2:15 once again, *Study to shew thyself approved unto God, a workman that needeth not to be ashamed, rightly dividing the Word of truth*. With knowledge comes

His power. With His power comes courage. With His courage comes victory.

> **Never apologize for being a Christian!**

Hellfighters must study, study, study. As a Hellfighter, you must learn as much as you can about our holy and righteous God. Don't wait; start now and by doing so you'll be able to introduce Jesus to everyone you meet without apology. But, don't be picky, tell everybody about Jesus.

ATTACK...
DON'T JUST DEFEND!

...Go ye into all the world, and preach the Gospel to every creature.

Mark 16:15b

RULE #5

Don't Pick and Choose

(Jesus paid too big a price for us to decide who can come.)

Riding motorcycles to Sturgis, South Dakota for our annual pilgrimage to the largest biker gathering on planet earth, we meet folks from all walks of life. The funny part is we have no idea if a guy on a Harley has 15¢ in his pocket or 15 G's, because everyone blends! The bikes are loud, the clothes are black, the hair is down and most women have as much skin exposed on the streets of Sturgis as they do in the privacy of their own homes. Why? Because on a Harley with the wind caressing your face, you are, for the moment, free from all the cares of the world and everyone is equal in the Harley circle of life.

During this event that, I must admit, we enjoy about as much as anything we do, we pass out thousands of tracts. We give them to the guys and gals who camp at Buffalo Chip, and we give them to the guys and gals who attend the rally in their $1 million Prevost motorhomes with their Harleys in-tow behind. We also give tracts to those in between these two stations of life.

On our way to the Sturgis Rally one year, our brakes failed and we had them repaired in the Laramie, Wyoming Harley shop. It took over three hours to get them fixed, but during that time we gave tracts to the mechanic and his helper, the shop owner and his wife, a guy from Phoenix who repairs golf clubs, the owner of the largest accounting firm in Wyoming and his best friend, who is president of the largest bank in Wyoming. Now here's the good part, if you had lined all these folks up, you couldn't have picked the banker out of the line-up to save your life. Why? Because they all looked the same.

When you come across someone you feel led to witness to, don't hesitate. Even though you don't have a clue what station in life they may be from, witness to them anyway. Who knows, the person you lead to Christ may become the world's last great evangelist. You may only lead one person to Christ in your whole life, but what if he or she is the one whom God has chosen to turn the world upside down for Him?

As I was writing this *Hellfighters Operations Manual*, I reflected on the tremendous flurry of controversy that surrounded a movie entitled *The Passion of the Christ*, back in 2004. It was produced and directed by Mel Gibson. Mel is a Hollywood superstar who makes tens of millions of dollars each year because of his acting and directing skills and unique personality.

The film that was in controversy is a scriptural account of the last twelve hours of Christ's life, which led up to and concluded with His crucifixion. The devil's crowd jumped on Mel's film with both feet; the Jewish crowd called Mel an anti-Semitist, the Christian community as a whole, however, applauded him. The skeptics called the film bloody, which it is. I'm not very smart, but even I know what crucifixion is all about. If it wasn't bloody the Scriptures would be in error when they say, they *...scourged Jesus* (Matthew 27:26), *...nailed Him to the cross* (Acts 2:23, NLT), and *...pierced His side with a spear* (John 19:34, NKJV). Matthew 27:26 emphasizes the cruelty of the crucifixion process, which was preceded by a brutal beating. *And when he* [Pilate] *had scourged Jesus, he delivered Him to be crucified.*

In the filming of *The Passion*, the actor who portrayed Christ had a *second skin* applied to his back. During the scourging scene, one of the strands of the "whip" containing embedded pieces of bone and metal, referred to by some as "the cat of nine tails," missed the *second skin* and actually hit the actor's body. The report said he would have a prominent scar for the rest of his life.

Now, here's my point. This record-breaking, box office hit awakened the masses to the reality and depth of Christ's love for them. This film caused many to investigate Jesus to see if He could be trusted. All who seek Him and find Him will agree that He can indeed be trusted.

Wouldn't you like to have been the guy who told Mel Gibson about Christ? Wouldn't it be a wonderful thing to know that you had been directly involved in the making of this powerful film? How would you like to know that you were directly involved in this powerful tool from *Hollywood* no less? You would already be a hero of the faith yourself just like those great and mighty men of valor found in the tribute chapter of Hebrews (Hebrews 11).

What if, however, you had been given the opportunity, but failed to tell that little ragamuffin kid from the trailer park about Christ and he had been Mel Gibson? What if you had failed to tell some kid in the $120 Tommy Hilfiger shirt about Christ, and he had been Mel Gibson? What if you had failed to tell some guitar-playing, baggy-pants-wearing, cigarette-smoking, drug-using, longhaired-hippie about Christ, and he had been Mel Gibson? What if you had failed to tell your own brother about Christ and he had been the anointed one to make *The Passion*? What if you don't tell *the one* about Jesus and countless millions go to hell because you copped out?

You see, this Jesus thing is a "you do your part and I'll do my part" exercise. If, however, I was lost, yet destined to be the last great evangelist and you were the one, chosen of God, to lead me to Christ, and you didn't do your part, I'd be very upset with you. I can't even begin to imagine how upset God would be with you. Let's not even go there shall we? Let's just commit ourselves to tell everyone we meet about Jesus and let the Holy Spirit do the rest.

Remember, we can't save anybody, we just make the introduction. We must also realize that it's not our privilege to pick and choose who deserves to hear or whom we think will accept our introduction. **The Gospel is for everyone**, because: *"God so loved the world, that He gave His only begotten Son, that whoever believes in Him shall not perish, but have eternal life"* (John 3:16, NASB). This is why we must introduce our featured guest, Jesus Christ, to everyone we meet, or know.

Remember, we don't do the saving, we just make the introduction. But to make that most important introduction we must be an open window of our faith.

Attack... Don't Just Defend!

Let your light so shine before men, that they may see your good works, and glorify your Father which is in Heaven.

Matthew 5:16

RULE #6

Be An Open Window

Hellfighters are sometimes guilty of putting our two cents into what we think the Scriptures really mean. I'm not saying we shouldn't. If God has given you an insight into the mysteries of a verse or passage, you should certainly share it. However, most people try to lead others to Christ and never use one Scripture verse. They say to the seeker, "There's a verse in the Bible that says something like this, blah, blah, blah." Listen, brother, this leading somebody to Jesus stuff is too important for you to make a haphazard, halfway attempt to share the content of a Scripture. So remember, *Study to shew thyself approved unto God, a workman that needeth not to be ashamed, rightly dividing the Word of truth* (2 Timothy 2:15).

Study the Scriptures, memorize the Scriptures, and practice quoting the Scriptures. But most importantly, share the Scriptures with those who are lost.

Read, study, and memorize the Scriptures.

If you can't recall the Scriptures, then you can't share the Scriptures. That's why it's important to learn as many Scripture verses as you can. Commit them to memory by writing them over and over. Practice quoting them to your friends or to your dog, if you have one. Make it a priority to become proficient with the Scriptures then you can't be accused of telling anyone an untruth.

As a Hellfighter, it's easy to tell everybody you meet what Jesus did for you, but to tell a lost person what Jesus can do for them, really needs to be backed up with Scripture.

Remember, most Hellfighters witness primarily to complete strangers who know absolutely nothing about Jesus or the Word of God. With them, you can sometimes "wing it" and get by. However, you must not be ill prepared, when you have the opportunity to share the Good News of Jesus Christ.

A Hellfighter must always remember that God's Word is the ultimate authority on the subject of salvation.

In the state of Mississippi, where Gina and I live, *Jesus* is a household word. There's a Bible on almost every coffee table in nearly every home in the Deep South, with four or five more Bibles or New Testaments scattered elsewhere throughout the house. I must confess that most of these Bibles aren't read like they should be. They were all purchased with good intentions, but the practicality of life and our inability to manage our time wisely have prevented most Mississippians, as well as most Americans, from reading our Bibles regularly.

We are from the *Bible belt* where there's a church on nearly every corner. The sad thing is a lot of them are lifeless or dying. Why? Because our moms, dads, grandmas and grandpas didn't keep up their end of the bargain with the One who saved them; they failed to raise their children God's way. The Bible encourages us to *Train up a child in the way he should go: and when he is old, he will not depart from it* (Proverbs 22:6). When we don't, we more than likely encounter serious problems.

In the small rural areas of our state, there are still some churches with windows that open, but because of air-conditioning, they remain closed. When I was a small boy, I remember walking to church with my mom and dad. We could hear Gospel music pouring out of the open windows of our church even before we got there. It was a peaceful sound, which filled the neighborhood with tranquility.

Today, most churches in America have closed their windows and succumbed to the demon of air-conditioning. Look at the new churches being constructed today. For the most part, they are windowless or have stained glass windows, which cannot be opened. Church architects, building committees and even pastors seem determined to keep the Gospel inside the church building.

Many pastors now call God's house a facility or a campus. Some call it a plant, but God's house is neither a plant nor a facility. Factories and flowers are plants; prisons and mental institutions are facilities. God's house is a place of worship, a house of prayer, a sanctuary of rest for the weary, a setting of solitude, a place of rejoicing and a lighthouse to the community. I cringe every time I hear God's house referred to as a plant or facility, don't you? I grew up calling the building where I went to church the *church house*. I think the name still fits.

The church's closed windows, the shallow commitment of its members, and the complacency of many pastors have led to the weakening of the fellowship of Believers. This has brought about a decline in the number of bold, knowledgeable soulwinners. We, who are the remnant so to speak, must be aware that this lost generation in which we live today is depending on us.

Hellfighters are the open windows to the lost. Hellfighters possess the tranquility that God wants others to have. Hellfighters possess the peace that passes all understanding, and He wants us to share this peace with others. Hellfighters are a lighthouse to the community in which we live. We are a beacon of hope to those in a darkened, sin-filled world.

Increasing our knowledge of the Word of God makes a Hellfighter's light shine brighter as our vibrant witness draws men toward God's haven of rest. Lack of study and lack of preparation will cause His light to weaken in us, and ultimately diminish into nothingness. A Hellfighter cannot be red-hot for Jesus one day and lukewarm the next. We must be red-hot all the time. But if you fail to study and pray regularly, you will become useless. No one is exempt from failing to be a good witness, not even a Hellfighter.

Were you once a beacon of hope for the lost, but now you've become a hopeless, lifeless, lightless beacon lacking the power to shine as you would like to? If your light for Christ once shined brightly, it can do so again. All you have to do is return to the precious Word of God, and ask Him to forgive you for your sorriness. Then ask Him to re-ignite that fire which once burned so brightly inside your heart.

If you've never been a soulwinner, you can become one. You can become that beacon of hope to lost family members and friends, as well as to those whom you've never met. You can be an outstanding Hellfighter if you want to be. It's up to you. God's power has your name on it, but you have to reach out and take it.

For the Word of God is quick, and powerful, and sharper then any twoedged sword, piercing even to the dividing asunder of soul and spirit, and of the joints and marrow, and is a discerner of the thoughts and intents of the heart (Hebrews 4:12). It's not what you say that brings men to Jesus; it's the power in the Word of God.

To be a good purveyor of God's Word takes time and prayer. Your training ground for knowledge is within the pages of God's Holy Word. Your battlefield, however, is the world. But before you endeavor to do battle for the souls of lost men you first must learn to pray properly.

GOD'S MODEL PRAYER

Our Father which art in Heaven,
Hallowed be Thy name. Thy kingdom come. Thy will be done in earth, as it is in Heaven. Give us this day our daily bread. And forgive us our debts, as we forgive our debtors. And lead us not into temptation, but deliver us from evil: For Thine is the kingdom, and the power, and the glory, for ever. Amen.
(Matthew 6:9-13)

Let this powerful prayer be your guide for a closer walk with the Lord, and don't forget to pray before you go witnessing. Touché!

ATTACK...
DON'T JUST DEFEND!

Evening, and morning, and at noon, will I pray, and cry aloud: and He shall hear my voice.

Psalm 55:17

RULE #7

Pray Before You Go

All across America we Christians have closed ourselves off from the world. Windowless churches keep the music and the Gospel in, half-hearted soulwinners consistently miss their opportunities to witness and church attendance continues to decline weekly. Why? Because most of us Christians won't pray like we should. I am sad to say that I too am guilty.

I do try to get in at least one hour of prayer and Bible study before I leave for work each day and, with few exceptions, I am able to do just that. However, I travel a lot, some for business and a lot for Jesus. Days on the road are long, nonstop, full-speed ahead, crammed as full as we can make them, and are, therefore, usually the hardest for me to spend time in prayer and Bible study because my routine gets broken. Oh, I say "Good morning, Lord" and I tell Him "Goodnight" on those hectic days, and I offer Him a prayer of thanks at mealtime, but anything other than that is oftentimes very difficult. On those days, however, I take advantage of small pockets of time between meetings or during a flight, even if it's only for ten minutes, to get my Bible out of my briefcase and spend time in the Word.

You can get all spiritual with me here and say, "If your prayer and Bible study life is no more intense than that, if you don't spend *hours* every day in prayer, why do you expect me to read anything you write?" Before I answer that, let me ask you a question, Bubba: "How consistent is your prayer and Bible study life?"

I honestly wish mine was better and I strive every day to make it so, but sometimes I put other things first, just like you do. But, that's no excuse for either of us not to pray regularly and read and study our Bible intently each and every day.

> As a child of God, prayer is like calling home everyday.

Early morning, around 4 a.m., is best for me. Gina, however, does her Bible study a little later, after I leave for work. We both read a little before bedtime, but most of the time late night Bible reading doesn't do much for me, I'm too tired. Our goodnight prayer, which is only four or five minutes long, is simply a good night love sonnet to our precious Lord and Savior, thanking Him for His blessings of the day.

This Rule, *Pray Before You Go*, was written while Gina and I were on "Jesus business" in Vietnam with Steve Waters, pastor of Patterson Springs Baptist Church in Grover, North Carolina; David and Sandy Cooper of Morganton, North Carolina; and Danny and Linda Stringer, from Indian Springs Baptist Church in Laurel, Mississippi. Danny is the missions pastor at his church, our dear friend and also senior pilot for our company.

During a long bus ride to a leper colony located in the Mekong River Delta of South Vietnam, our team discussed the emphasis on prayer in the Vietnamese church, and the lack of it in the American church. We then discussed the intensity and power of prayer in the Vietnamese underground church. The majority of the members in the underground church fast three days each month. Some of these individuals fast one additional day each week. They take the Bible literally when it speaks of the power, which comes from prayer and fasting.

Steve and I were talking later that same day about how many of America's churches have taken the Wednesday night prayer service and turned it into a mid-week worship service, with an opening and closing prayer, rather than having a service with an emphasis on prayer. Many Wednesday night services have been watered down to consist only of a pastor's class, youth service, weight loss seminar, knitting class, or worse than that, many have been cancelled altogether.

Steve's church, however, is different. He has Wednesday night prayer meetings the old-fashioned way. His people, young and old alike, assemble together and pray and pray and pray. Steve attributes his church's stability and its growth to the faithful prayer life of his members and especially to the Wednesday night prayer service.

A Hellfighter's life should be so saturated with communication to and from our Heavenly Father that we feel His power all the time. As Hellfighters, we should bathe ourselves in prayer everyday, so that we may be filled with the sweet Heavenly fragrance of Christ that will draw men to Him through us.

Neither your prayer life nor my prayer life will ever be what God would like them to be, unless... we *desire* to have a great prayer life and then *strive* to make it so. God will bless the desires of our heart, and says so in Psalm 37:4, *Delight thyself also in the LORD; and He shall give thee the desires of thine heart.*

When the opportunity presents itself for you to witness to someone, ask God for guidance.

Seek His help in knowing just how to make *the introduction*. Then pray, brother, pray!

I'm really bad about doing stuff without consulting God first. Of course, I know you never do that, now do you? Sure you do and so do 99% of all of us who profess Christ as our Savior and Lord. As an air-breathing human, you probably think you have all the answers to everything, just like I do. If so, you get ahead of God and more than likely mess things up, just like I do. This means we should pray, brother, pray!

In most cases, you can repair or mend your zealous actions of doing things on your own, but... when it comes to a soul you best be careful not to get ahead of God. If you mess up introducing Jesus to a lost person, you may be directly responsible for the eternal damning of that soul. This is why prayer is so important. So, pray, brother, pray!

Pray and pray and pray some more before you witness to someone. If you will, then God will set your lips afire with words of wisdom, and Scripture will flow as poetry. Remember, you cannot save anyone, Jesus Himself does that, but you are the introducer of the Redeemer, and your introduction must be flawless.

I know all this may scare you into not wanting to witness at all, especially if you're not prayed up and studied up. But, if you love Jesus, it doesn't matter if you can't read or write, or if you stutter when you talk, God can still use you, IF...you have a desire to be used.

The next time you feel like God can't use you, just remember: Noah was a drunk; Abraham was too old; Isaac was a daydreamer; Jacob was a liar; Leah was ugly; Joseph was abused; Moses had a stuttering problem; Gideon was afraid; Samson was a womanizer; Rahab was a prostitute; Jeremiah and Timothy were too young; David had an affair and was a murderer; Elijah was suicidal; Isaiah preached naked; Jonah ran from God; Naomi was a widow; Job went bankrupt; Peter denied Christ; the disciples fell asleep while praying; Martha worried about everything; the Samaritan woman was divorced, more than once; Zacchaeus was too small; Paul was too religious; Timothy had an ulcer... AND Lazarus was dead!

Now! No more excuses! God can use you to your full potential. Besides you aren't the message, you're just the messenger.

Over the years, many Christians have told me they were unable to quote Scripture and didn't know very much about the Bible, yet they still wanted to tell others about Jesus. Their question was, "How can I lead someone to Christ if I don't know how?" My answer is always simply this, "Tell them what Jesus did for you."

I know I said earlier that we should back up our introduction of Jesus with Scripture, but neither me, you, nor anyone else should restrict someone from telling people about Jesus, regardless of how little Scripture they may know. The only criteria anyone must meet before they can witness is they *must be born again* (John 3:7).

O'Farrell Whatley, a former hell-bound reprobate, Special Forces soldier and recently born again Christian, told more people about Christ the first week he got saved than most Christians tell in a lifetime.

Should O'Farrell have been forbidden to tell others about Jesus because he had just met Him?

Heavens, no! O'Farrell didn't know hardly anything about Jesus the day he got saved, but that didn't stop him. He prayed for courage and then told everybody he met what God had so miraculously done for Him. He has matured a lot since then in Scriptural knowledge and he has also learned about the power of prayer, nevertheless, O'Farrell was a Hellfighter from day one.

It's nice to be knowledgeable of God's Word! And, if the Holy Spirit dwells in you, He will take care of each and every situation, as it becomes necessary for Him to do so.

Pray, study, and **tell!** These are the three ingredients for effective soulwinning. Read the following questions and see how you respond:

1. Did you **PRAY** fervently today?

   YES ☐ NO ☐

2. Did you **STUDY** the Bible intently today?

   YES ☐ NO ☐

3. Did you **TELL** anyone about Jesus today?

   YES ☐ NO ☐

4. Will your tomorrow be the same as your today?

   YES ☐ NO ☐

You can mark it down, brother, tomorrow your life will be filled with either victories and satisfaction or defeats and disappointment. It's up to you to decide which ones will prevail in your life.

Even when you're prepared, soulwinning won't be easy. Remember, Satan hates your guts and he will hinder you and cause you to fail even when you think you're doing the right thing. Be alert and be sensitive to the leadership of the Holy Spirit. Do your soulwinning the Bible way, not your way. Remember, Jesus does the saving; you are just the introducer. Never try to force anyone into having a salvation experience by being a spiritual gunslinger. Just plant the seeds and let God give the increase.

Pray, study, then tell!

ATTACK...

DON'T JUST DEFEND!

So then neither he who plants is anything, nor he who waters, but God who gives the increase.

1 Corinthians 3:7 (NKJV)

RULE #8

Don't Become a Spiritual Gunslinger

A friend of mine went on a mission trip to New York City a few years back to distribute Bibles. Late one night his team was returning to their hotel on a chartered bus. Passing a crowd of bystanders on the corner of a busy intersection, my friend took handfuls of Bibles and tossed them into the crowd. Some of them hit people in the head, chest and arms. Some of them fell to the ground and slid wastefully into the gutters. I know his intentions were good, but I'm sure those who were *beaten up* by this type *presentation* of the Word of God were not very impressed.

We used to own a hotel in Centennial, Wyoming called The Old Corral. It was built in 1876 as a rest stop for early pioneers. This is where a friend of ours was working when we bought the place. He is a delightful man in his late seventies and has one of the grandest personalities we've ever encountered.

Over the years, we've told our friend many times about Jesus and the peace that is available to him through Jesus Christ. Each time, our friend would moan and groan and tell us that he knew he should change, but just wasn't ready to mend his ways. He would go to church with us from time to time, but did so only after great encouragement from us and others. I felt that time, our faithful witness and our continual loving on him would eventually bring him to Jesus.

However, some gung-ho holier-than-thous showed up at our hotel one day and cornered our friend on the front porch while he was smoking a cigarette. You talk about a high pressure pitch, these guys hammered on our friend in front of his peers and our hotel guests alike. He later told me,

"I prayed the prayer they wanted me to pray just to get rid of them."

This ain't soulwinning! This is spiritual harassment and nothing will come out of this kind of soulwinning effort, except horror stories.

Would you like to hear the rest of the story of our friend's "front porch conversion"? I would love to tell you that Heaven came down and the glory of God filled his life, that he is now one of Centennial's finest Christians and a soulwinning machine, but I can't. This high-pressure soulwinning tactic turned him away from the church. These spiritual gunslingers turned this experience into a mockery of God and not only turned our friend away from God, but away from us also. He resigned his position at our hotel and now hangs out in one of the local bars wasting his life away and smoking himself to death. How tragic!

> **God wants spiritual fruit, not religious nuts.**

We had tilled the soil of our friend's soul and planted the spiritual seeds of Christ's love in his heart, but two Hellfighter-wannabes were dead set on putting a notch on their spiritual six shooters. Because of their "beat 'em into submission" concept of soulwinning, they blew the deal and possibly damned a soul to an eternity in hell.

When I witness to some-one, I am normally too soft. I believe, however, with all my heart that the Holy Spirit will take over where I leave off and bring about the harvest of that soul. There is a balance in the art of soulwinning, but it is sometimes hard to find. It blends the way, the truth and the life of a real soulwinner with the zealous exuberance of a spiritual gunslinger.

> **Remember, seeds only grow on fertile ground.**

A lady named Le is one of those gifted soul-winners who has found that perfect balance. She is a liaison between our charitable foundations and several Vietnamese orphanages and lepro-sariums in Central and Southern Vietnam. We met Le on our first trip to Saigon in 1996 and have worked with her in aiding lepers and orphaned Vietnamese children ever since.

When we are in Vietnam, even though our mission work begins early each day and extends into the night, we always find time to shop for souvenirs and Christmas gifts. One shop we frequent in downtown Saigon, which is now called Ho Chi Minh City, is *Suong Silk*. It is owned by a local family and run by the owners' children Ngoc Chau, Lán, Lanh, Hien and Hieu.

We actually feel like their family is part of our family. We cry with happiness when we see them upon our arrival in Saigon and we cry with sadness when we leave them to come home. We love them! They love us too because they have seen our hearts in action. We have told them for years about our personal relationship with Jesus and how it's because of Him that we are always happy. It is also because of Him that we love each of them as we do and it is because of Him that we go to Vietnam. We have given them tracts, the *Jesus* film, and other Christian literature, but we've never been pushy. We've just been faithful and planted Gospel seeds.

However, in 2003, October 6, my *biological* birthday, became their *spiritual* birthday! That Monday morning, three of the sisters, Ngoc Chau, Lanh, and Hien came to our hotel to bring some of our merchandise we had purchased at their shop the day before and to bring me a birthday gift. Ngoc Chau, pronounced *Nup Chow*; Lanh, which rhymes with *man*; and Hien, pronounced like the chicken that lays eggs, sat down with us. I didn't know it yet, but this day was going to be different. We were having a strategy meeting with Le concerning a leper colony located an hour or so outside Saigon. As the three sisters listened to our discussion of the day's upcoming activities, they asked in broken English, "Why do you do so much for our people?"

Le took over from there and began to tell them in their language that Jesus lived in our hearts, and because of His love for us, we loved the Vietnamese people.

They asked more questions, Le gave more answers and then she asked them, "Would you like to let Jesus come live in your heart?" To our amazement they excitedly responded in succession, "Yes, Yes, Yes!"

Tears filled my eyes, Gina's eyes, and the eyes of our team members as Le began to lead them in the repentant sinner's prayer. I couldn't believe it. Everything happened so quickly that day, yet it took seven years of our showing them and their family God's love. From 1996 to 2003 seems like a long time, but in the whole of it all, it was just a blink of an eye.

We saw Ngoc Chau, Lanh and Hien the following day and their whole countenance had changed; their hair seemed more beautiful, their faces appeared fresher, even their clothes looked like they fit better. These were new creations, refined to perfection by the marvelous grace of God.

Over the years, God has allowed us to plant spiritual seeds all across America and around the world, but often times He allows others to reap the bountiful harvests.

Would I have liked to have been the one to lead Ngoc Chau, Lanh and Hien to Christ? Absolutely, but it was not to be. Why? For one thing, I'm not Vietnamese—Le is. Second, I don't speak Vietnamese and if I had tried leading them to Christ while Le translated, something could have been misinterpreted or misunderstood. But with Le speaking in her native language, she gracefully led these three precious ladies to the throne room of God where Jesus Himself was waiting to receive them.

The bag of salted peanuts they gave me that morning as a birthday present was a wonderful gift, but them accepting Christ was the best birthday present I'll ever receive. Now I know that even more of our little Vietnamese friends will spend their eternity with us in Heaven with Jesus. We are praying that their sisters, Lán and Hieu, will accept Christ also.

Jesus says in 1 Corinthians 3:6-8, that if we will be faithful to plant and water the seeds, He, and He alone, will give the increase.

You may not harvest all the souls of those in whom you plant the spiritual seeds of the Gospel, but that's OK. God uses some of us to plant the seeds, others to cultivate and some to harvest. It takes all of us, doing what God has gifted each of us to do for Him to get the job done.

Exercise your gifts and don't hold anything back. Give every lost person you meet a dose of buckshot Gospel, but don't try to force someone into having a salvation experience. It can't be done. Only Jesus can save. He'll use you to point men to Him, He'll use the Holy Spirit to soften their hearts, but Jesus and Jesus alone is the only One who can redeem lost souls from hell. He paid the price to redeem the souls of the lost. Only He can receive them unto Himself.

Be bold, but don't be pushy. Be firm, but not overbearing. Be loving and smile a lot. Soulwinning is serious business, but it should not have the trappings of a funeral dirge. Don't push someone into making a decision that does not come from their heart. You may push them away from God as the over zealous, holy-roller gunslingers did to our friend in Wyoming. You could mislead them into believing that they got saved, when in actuality they didn't. This will take them straight to hell.

There's an old saying down South that goes like this, "You can lead a horse to water, but you can't make him drink." Only the sweet fragrance of God's love draws the repentant sinner into the throne room of His saving grace. It's up to you to show them the way. Don't let your bad breath deny them the privilege!

ATTACK...
DON'T JUST DEFEND!

[Moses] set the laver between the tabernacle of meeting and the altar, and put water there for washing; and Moses, Aaron and his sons would wash their hands and their feet with water from it. Whenever they went into the tabernacle of meeting, and when they came near the altar, they washed, as the Lord had commanded Moses.

Exodus 40:30-32

RULE #9

Brush Your Teeth

Have you ever tried to be romantic with someone who had bad breath? Have you ever kissed someone with bad breath? Ugh! Have you ever smelled her armpits? If you have, you need to tell that gal to take a bath.

Have you lain face to face with your spouse after having been asleep for eight hours? The exhales are not quite as refreshing as they were when you kissed each other goodnight, huh? So, before you wake your wife, dude, go brush your teeth! I get up early and brush my teeth twice before I wake Gina. Why? Because I love her and I don't want to breathe bad breath on her.

Bad breath is not very romantic is it? Soulwinning, visitation and church attendance also require that our breath be fresh and our deodorant active. Nothing will turn a prospect off faster than over zealous pressure, bad breath or body odor.

It doesn't cost 5¢ to brush your teeth and dab a little underarm deodorant on before you go. If you don't and your seeker keeps backing away from you, take the hint, keep your arms down and don't exhale until you're done.

I know a couple of people who have bad breath and they get right up in my face when they want to tell me something. I have actually found myself holding my breath while they talk.

It's true that some folks have halitosis. This is a bodily disorder that causes them to have horrible breath, regardless of what hygiene precautions they may take. These folks are exceptions and chances are you are not one of them, which means if you have bad breath it's from sorriness.

I invented a shirt pocket toothbrush long ago that businessmen could carry like a fountain pen. It would have been perfect for brushing one's teeth after lunch, but I never did anything with my idea. Now the world is still plagued with millions of people who have pepper grinds or grits between their teeth while breathing their garlic-reeking breath on others—some of whom are lost.

We Hellfighters don't want to do that, now do we? Certainly not. That's why we should brush after every meal and sometimes in between. We should also carry breath mints, or those pungent little breath strips, for emergencies.

The Bible says in 1 Peter 2:9 that, we are to be a peculiar people. I think God means that in a good way. I think He wants us to be clean and smelling good. Rejoicing that we are also clean on the inside, we should acknowledge Him as our washing machine.

There's an old song, which goes something like this, *"Whiter than snow, Lord, wash me just now, as in Thy presence, humbly I bow."*

Isn't it wonderful to know that everyone can be washed in the soul-cleansing blood of the Lamb and that our lives can be spotless and our hearts purer than snow? Yes, and that's why it is important that we understand that people, who sincerely desire God's cleansing, could be turned off by something so simple as bad breath and body odor. Take five minutes to tidy up then go out and speak up. It's a simple rule, but one of utmost importance. Personal hygiene is easy to maintain in America and unless you're a sorry, nasty and uncaring person, you will want to do your part in this often under prioritized area of soulwinning.

I said all this to point out how every aspect of our lives matters when we are introducing Christ to someone. We don't want to do anything to distract or detract from His Good News.

Do all you can do for the glory of God. He doesn't care about your abilities. He only wants your availability. If you will make yourself available to Him, He will present some awesome opportunities to you. When they come along, DO NOT fail to take advantage of each one. DO NOT procrastinate when it comes to Jesus business!

ATTACK... DON'T JUST DEFEND!

…BEHOLD, NOW IS THE ACCEPTED TIME; BEHOLD, NOW IS THE DAY OF SALVATION.

2 CORINTHIANS 6:2B

RULE #10

Don't Put It Off

It's not a good idea to wait to tell your friends about Jesus. Reflect back and you'll immediately recall a loved one, a friend, or an acquaintance who has already passed on into eternity whom you never told about the saving grace of Jesus.

Where are they now—Heaven or hell? Did God allow someone else to tell them about Jesus before they died? If so, you can rejoice with them in Heaven when you get there. If not, their blood is on your hands. Ezekiel 3:18 (NKJV) confirms, *"When I say to the wicked 'You shall surely die,' and you give him no warning, nor speak to warn the wicked from his wicked way, to save his life, that same wicked man shall die in his iniquity; but his blood I will require at your hand."*

Was one of your dead friends or acquaintances the chosen one; the last great evangelist; the one who would have led millions to Christ before His return? If this were the case, I'd hate to be in your shoes, brother!

I have some failures that I vividly remember and I regret them all. As Gina and I have traveled the length and breadth of this country and to parts of over 80 other countries, we have distributed hundreds of thousands of tracts and felt God's pleasure each time we've passed one out.

I'm the first to admit that I can't remember the faces of all the folks who have taken our tracts; I do, however, remember many faces of the folks who rejected them. Toll booth operators on our nation's toll roads, park rangers and sundry other government employees are the worst offenders. They rarely accept them and when they do, they do so reluctantly. Even though our government was founded on Christian principles, most of our government officials seem to be sympathetic to every religion except Christianity. I am saddened every time I think of how our government hates the things of God. And when compared to our Founding Fathers' love for Jesus, it is heartbreaking.

Even big businessmen sometimes consider it an insult if they think I think they may be lost. I have given tracts to folks who took them, wadded them up, and while looking me square in the face, threw them on the ground. I have had men raise their fists at me in anger and say through gritted teeth, "I'm not interested in any of 'that stuff'!"

I remember countless others to whom I failed in my introduction attempt of Jesus. I can live with these failed attempts. What I have a hard time living with are the memories of the faces of those to whom I never even tried: that black construction worker sitting on a five-gallon bucket, that Hell's Angel in Sturgis, that Satan's Disciple at the Memorial Day Blowout on the

Mississippi Gulf Coast, that deacon who called the cops on me...

I remember my friends John, Cheryl, Mike, David, Joel and the man who detailed my truck, whose name I never knew. Oh yes, I remember them alright, but what good is a memory when I know in my heart they're in hell? Why do I think they're in hell? Because I put off telling them about Jesus.

> **A Hellfighter finds a way. A counterfeit Christian... an excuse!**

Are you guilty? Sure you are! We all are. Oh, God forgive us!

You see, I could be the one who failed to lead the last great evangelist to Christ. Was the black guy sitting on the five-gallon bucket that I passed hastily on my way to the Southern Baptist Convention in Atlanta *the one*? Was the Hell's Angel I failed to witness to in Sturgis, because I was afraid, *the one*? Was Charlie, the guy who couldn't read the tract I gave him at the gas station in Fort Collins, *the one*? Was it John, the architect? Was it Dennis the insurance salesman? Was it David the painter, Bill the mechanic, Matt the lawyer, Philip the waiter, Nick the cook or Andrew the doctor? Was the last great evangelist any one of the thousands of other lost people to whom I've failed to witness?

The list goes on and on because even as a Hellfighter I'm guilty of "putting it off." It's so easy to say, "I'll talk to them about Jesus... later." However, at one point in my life, I was where most Hellfighter-wannabes are today—I *couldn't* tell anybody about Jesus because I was a counterfeit Christian. Oh yeah, I went to church, ushered, became a deacon, and even served as a trustee. I taught Sunday School and, believe it or not, preached on Sunday. Yet I was as lost as a goose! I dressed like a Christian. I smelled like a Christian, I did those things that a Christian is supposed to do, but I had no peace within because I had never met the Peace Giver. I knew about Him, but I did not know Him personally.

In those days, I wanted to believe I was saved, but deep down I knew there was something wrong. I always felt a little tug in my heart when an invitation for the lost to be saved was given. I would always repeat the sinner's prayer because I wanted to "cover my bases." Have you ever done that? If so, you had better give this chapter some serious thought. Because if something feels wrong, it usually is.

However, in 1989, Jesus took up residence in my life and gave me the power I needed to become a Hellfighter. He'll do the same for you if you'll quit faking it and get right with God. **Please, don't put it off!**

You may not be lost. You may be saved, but you're just a cackling, chicken Christian, a Hellfighter-wannabe. If so, stop your cackling and start living the Christ-like life. Then and only then will He fill you with His power. Psalm 81:10b (NKJV) says, ... *Open your mouth wide, and I will fill it.* Matthew 4:19b says, ...*I will make you fishers of men.* John 1:12 says, *But as many as received Him, to them gave He* [the] *power to become the sons of God, even to them that believe on His name.* Then and only then can you fulfill the battle cry of the Hellfighter that should resound daily from your lips—LET'S GO GETTUM!

If you're lost, will you wait until it's too late to be saved? Will you wait until it's too late to submit your whole being to the One who died for you? Will you wait as millions grope in darkness waiting for the light that only you can give? Will you be the one who leads the last great evangelist to Christ? If it's not me who has this privilege, then I hope it's you, and if it is, I hope you will! But before you can, you must have peace with God.

This *Hellfighters Operations Manual* is intended mainly for those who are born again and I want to believe you are. If, however, you have the least little doubt about your salvation being secure, get it straight right now by accepting Jesus as your Savior and letting Him become your Lord.

I don't have to tell you what to say, you already know. You didn't get this far by being ignorant of God's Word. All that's left for you to do, if you believe you're lost, is to sincerely repent and ask God to save you and He will.

The next step is to ask Jesus what He wants you to do for Him. I bet I know what He'll say, "Son, be a Hellfighter and start introducing Me to all your lost friends." Who knows, you may be the

...he that winneth souls is wise.

PROVERBS 11:30B

one to lead the last great evangelist to Christ. But on the other hand, YOU MAY BE THE LAST GREAT EVANGELIST! If you are, what are you going to do about it? Selah!

ATTACK... DON'T JUST DEFEND!

Give me understanding, and I shall keep Thy law; yea, I shall observe it with my whole heart.

Psalm 119:34

Remembering the Rules

RULE # 1

Remember to treat Jesus Christ with reverence and love. We must give Him our best, not our leftovers.

RULE # 2

Remember that you aren't the one who's going to do the saving of those you talk to about Jesus. Knowing that soulwinning is spiritual warfare and that Satan hates your guts, let the Holy Spirit help you engage the enemy. He's battle-ready and a proven warrior.

RULE # 3

Remember that you're a spokesperson for the great I Am. Be a good one!

RULE # 4

Remember that only a Coca-Cola Christian, aka "The Real Thing," can qualify to become a Hellfighter.

RULE # 5

Remember that the one person you fail to witness to could be America's *last great evangelist*.

RULE # 6

Remember that you're not the ultimate authority—God's Word is.

RULE # 7

Remember to pray before you tell someone about Jesus.

RULE # 8

Remember that you can't beat 'em into submission.

RULE # 9

Remember to brush your teeth and use good deodorant.

RULE # 10

Remember to tell people about Jesus Christ *right now* so you won't have any regrets later.

Be sober, be vigilant; because your adversary the devil, as a roaring lion, walketh about, seeking whom he may devour.

1 Peter 5:8

Epilogue

There are other *Operations Manuals* in the Hellfighter series. Volume three, entitled *The Conflict of a Hellfighter,* is required reading for every Hellfighter. It describes the challenges that confront a Hellfighter's faith. It reveals how far you've come in your Christian walk and that there is no turning back for you now. It proves whether or not you've been called into God's league of extraordinary ladies and gentlemen and whether or not your name is synonymous with Christian warfare. If so, Satan will not rest until you are incapacitated or dead.

Be alert! Once you become a serious threat to him he will send a deluge of temptations and stumbling blocks before you. So, be strong and fear not. Reinforce your faith by putting on the whole armor of God.

You will need every resource available to you to defeat Satan's onslaught. The Bible is your supply depot. All the weapons and ammunition you need to defeat Satan are there, you just have to study and retrieve them. Properly prepared, you will succeed.

> **Put on the whole armour of God, that ye may be able to stand against the wiles of the devil.**
>
> EPHESIANS 6:11

Hellfighters Operations Manual 3: The Conflict of a Hellfighter will reveal to you the level of faith, courage and commitment you now have. It will also reveal the level of your willingness to use them in the conflict that Satan will bring against you. *The Conflict of a Hellfighter* will confirm to you that the ultimate victory in your battle with Satan is yours. You must realize that he is mankind's greatest foe, but it's up to *you* to let him know that you are his worst nightmare! So, com'on Hellfighter—LET'S GO GETTUM!

ATTACK…
DON'T JUST DEFEND!

PUT ON
THE WHOLE
ARMOUR
OF GOD, THAT
YE MAY BE ABLE
TO STAND
AGAINST THE
WILES OF THE
DEVIL.

EPHESIANS 6:11

About the Author

Richard Headrick is a successful businessman whose passion is writing encouraging and thought provoking books for Christians and Christian-wannabes.

See the following pages for a list of products by Richard Headrick.

Richard has written many books, including:

The Well

The Circular Rings of Kansas

Poor Richard's Proverbs

The Treasures of Solomon

A Redneck's Guide to Financial Freedom

Goliath's Fall

America's Churches through the Eyes of a Bum

Hellfighters Operations Manual 1: The Call of a Hellfighter

Hellfighters Operations Manual 3: The Conflict of a Hellfighter

The Enemy of Heaven

The Seven Churches

My Other Little Book on The Seven Churches

Love Letters from a King

God, If We're the Best You've Got, You're in Big Trouble

Why Everybody Needs Jesus

Richard has also written Gospel tracts, including:

Richard the Rhino Man

Hellfighters

Have a Great Day!

Orangevestitis

Will Someone Plant a Tree for You?

Something Special

Guardian Angels

Is Hell Right for You?

There's Only One Thing Better Than a Hummer

In the Company of Fish

The War Wagon

Nickel Tissue

The World is Ablaze

Keeping Christ in Christmas

I'm Here for the Party!

SATAN SUCKS

Some books and tracts are out of print, but may still be available through various sources. Go to www.hellfighters.org or send us an e-mail to info@hellfighters.org to order these books and other items that are available. If we've got it in stock, then you've got it. If we don't have it, we'll tell you who may have it and where you might be able to get it. If nobody has 'em, it means you've waited too late and missed out.

It's OK to miss out on these books, but don't mess around and miss out on Heaven.

Other Hellfighter Productions

Keeping Christ in Christmas – audio CD

Christians Still Die – DVD

Last Ounce of Courage - DVD

Heaven's sweet.
Hell's hot.
You're going to one.
Ready or not!

HELLFIGHTER PUBLICATIONS
One Freedom Square
Laurel, MS 39440-3367
601-649-HOPE (4673)
www.hellfighters.org
info@hellfighters.org

To Be Continued…

Now that you've read the rules of how to be an effective Hellfighter, the question is, "Will you pay the price to be one?" *Hellfighters Operations Manual 3: The Conflict of a Hellfighter* will show you in great detail what Satan will use to defeat you unless you follow the way of the Master.

Read On!

Glossary of Terms

Accepting Jesus – Denouncing Satan and placing one's trust in Jesus Christ.

Blessed Assurances – Slang for a person's backside.

Blood on Your Hands – If a saved person knows a lost person and doesn't tell him about the saving grace of Jesus Christ and that lost person dies and goes to hell, the person who knew the truth about salvation, but didn't share it, will be found guilty by God and the blessings due him will be withheld. Example: The lost person's blood will be on his hands.

Buckshot Gospel – Instead of using just one Scripture to lead someone to Christ, a soulwinner will use many verses to make his point.

Cackling, Chicken Christian – A saved person who talks big in the circles of other Believers, but is afraid to take the truths of the Gospel to the neglected areas and people of our world.

Camp Meeting – In the early days of our country, congregations of Christians would hold revival services outside the confines of the four walls of their church. A shelter would be built of limbs, lumber and sometimes even a tent would be used. People would come from miles around. Some would come for one day; others would camp for the duration of the services, thus the name camp meeting. Visiting preachers and evangelists would speak of Jesus during these services.

Christ's Mysteries – The truths of the Gospel of Jesus Christ that are not easily understood.

Christ-Like Life – Christ was the only perfect person who ever lived on planet earth. Our goal, as a Christian, should be to pattern our life after Him.

Church House – A building that is occupied by Believers in Jesus Christ for the purpose of prayer, praise and worship.

Commission – An edict, command or authorization to carry out a mission given by a person or a commander in chief.

Countenance – The look on one's face that shows happiness or sadness.

Counterfeit Christian – A person who pretends to be saved, but really isn't.

Creator – God.

Demon of A/C – A slang expression that puts the blame of the comforts of air-conditioning on the A/C unit itself.

Devilish Cults – Those religions with teachings contrary to the teachings of Jesus Christ.

Eternal Damning – Those who reject Jesus will be found guilty and sentenced to hell forever and ever. Some Scriptures refer to this as damnation.

Gabriel – The archangel of Heaven, a.k.a. the gatekeeper, or business manager of Heaven.

God's Forever Family – A group comprised of those human beings who have put their total trust in Jesus Christ.

God's Haven of Rest – The eternal home in Heaven that Believers in Jesus Christ receive upon their death.

God's Word – The Bible.

God's Holy Word – The Bible.

Gospel Seeds – Verses of Scripture; stories and truths from the Bible, God's Holy Word.

Grope in Darkness – As a person who endeavors to maneuver in an unlit building encounters difficulties, so does a lost person who exists in his sinful state of unrighteousness and meaningless living. Only the Light of Jesus will penetrate the darkness and help the lost find their way.

Harvest of a Soul – This simply means a lost person has been saved.

Heaven – The place where those who place their trust in Jesus Christ will live forever after they die. It is a wonderful place.

Heavenly Father – God.

Heavenly Thrift Store – Many people think God is the great, benevolent guru and expects Him to give anything to anybody who asks, for free.

Hell – The place where those who reject Jesus Christ and His guidelines for righteous living will live forever after they die. It is a horrible place of pain, punishment and eternal separation from God.

Hell-Bound Sinner – Any lost person who continues to reject Christ's redemptive plan for their life.

Hellfighter's Light – An attitude. A presence that reflects the love of God.

Hellfighter-Wannabe – A Christian who wants something more from the Christian experience than warming a pew on Sunday morning.

Hellfire/Damnation Preaching – Hard, Scripture-based preaching that confirms the penalties of sin.

His Good News – The Holy Bible.

Holier Than Thou – A person who thinks they know everything there is to know about God and wants everyone to know it. A self-righteous person.

Holy Roller - A person who thinks they know everything there is to know about God and wants everyone to know it. A self-righteous person.

Holy Spirit Dwelling in You – The radiating presence of the Holy Spirit guiding your life.

Hound of Heaven – Jesus Christ will never give up on a lost person; therefore, He is kind of like a bloodhound on the trail of an escaped convict.

Jehovah – God

Jesus Business – Doing things that point to Christ; preaching; caring for those in need; writing Christian literature; giving to the poor; witnessing to the lost, etc.

Last Great Evangelist – I believe God will give the world one more chance to repent and come to the knowledge of His saving grace. It will take one God-led, God-anointed, God-appointed servant of God to orchestrate this grand finale. This person will come from the rank and file of those who love Jesus with all their heart, mind, soul and strength.

Lips Afire – A slang expression describing a born again Believer who can't keep his mouth shut about Jesus.

Lost – *adjective* - The condition of a person who disbelieves in Jesus Christ and is therefore bound for hell. Example: He is lost because he has not trusted Jesus Christ. *noun* – Those persons who reject Jesus Christ and are sentenced to an eternity in hell because of their unbelief. Example: We must lead the lost to Christ.

Lost Generation – Young and old alike who have rejected Jesus and have chosen to serve Satan.

Michael – The archangel of Heaven, aka the warring angel.

Noah's Generation – A time long ago, when men and women rebelled against God and caused Him to destroy mankind. Very similar to the day and age we're living in now.

Omnipotent – Unlimited ability. A characteristic belonging only to God. There is absolutely nothing he cannot do.

Omnipresent – The ability to be everywhere all the time. A characteristic belonging only to God.

Peace Giver – Jesus.

Plain Jane Christian – The everyday, run-of-the-mill Christian who goes to church on Sunday morning, says a goodnight prayerette and grace over meals and thinks they're living the Christ-like life. A Christian who has never experienced the joy of what serving Jesus is really about.

Plant the Seeds of the Gospel – Simply telling others about the Gospel of Jesus Christ.

Putting on the New Man – The cleansing process of salvation; resigning one's self to putting God first and leaving old habits and sinful ways behind.

Redeemer – Jesus Christ.

Repentant Sinner's Prayer – Sometimes referred to as the "sinner's prayer," it is a prayer of a lost person who resigns himself to the fact that Jesus is the only one who can forgive sins and save lives.

Salvation Experience – The act of getting saved; being born again; being snatched from Satan's grasp; putting on the new man.

Satan – Father of lies, master of deceit, ruler of darkness, destroyer of men's souls, the evil one.

Saved – *noun* - Anyone who has placed their trust in Jesus Christ and knows in their heart that Jesus is the One and only Son of God and that by His Grace we are saved. *verb* – What Jesus did when you put your trust in Him. Example: Jesus saved me.

Saving Grace – The merciful favor of God that allows a sinful person to reject sin and become a member of God's forever family.

Scaredy Cat Club – Christians who are afraid to testify about what Jesus did for them and can do for you, aka cowards!

Seeds of the Gospel - Verses of Scripture; stories and truths from the Bible, God's Holy Word.

Sodom and Gomorrah – Two cities of ancient times that rejected God and chose to follow the unrighteous ways of Satan. God destroyed these cities because of their blatant disregard for the holiness of God.

Son of Man – Jesus.

Soul-Cleansing Blood – The Bible says, the only thing that can wash away or cleanse us from our sins is the blood of Jesus, which He shed during his sacrificial death on the cross. This act of obedience by Christ Himself is referred to as the blood sacrifice. Example: Jesus shed His blood for us. In other words, He gave His life for us.

Soulwinner – A Christian who leads a lost person to Christ.

Soulwinning – The act of an individual Christian, or group of Christians, who leads lost people to Christ.

Spiritual Gunslinger – A person who sets his sights on a lost person and becomes somewhat forceful in their presentation of the Gospel.

Spiritual Seeds - Verses of Scripture; stories and truths from the Bible, God's Holy Word.

Spiritual Warfare – The forces of good and evil are at war. We cannot see them, except in unusual circumstances, but the angels of Heaven are in constant conflict with the demons of hell over the souls of men and the control of earth itself.

The Great I Am – The One and Only God of the universe.

The Mysteries of the Gospel – The truths of the Gospel of Jesus Christ that are not easily understood.

Throne Room of God – A Heavenly destination where God resides.

Underground Church – In some countries, it is unlawful to profess your faith in Jesus Christ publicly, consequently Believers meet in secret. In ancient times, these secret meetings were first held in caves and underground facilities to avoid detection by the authorities.

Visitation - A time set aside each week when members of a church gather and go door to door in their community telling folks about Jesus.

Witness – *verb* – The act of telling someone what Jesus has done for you. *noun* – One who has seen or heard something. A person whose experience serves as evidence. A Christian who reflects Christ in everything they do.

Word of God – The Bible.